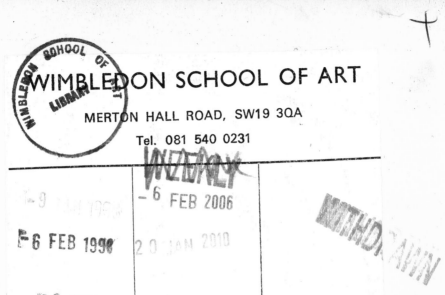

GOYA
The Disparates

National Touring Exhibitions

sbc

A National Touring Exhibition organised by the Hayward Gallery, London

Exhibition organised by Roger Malbert, assisted by Julia Risness
Education material prepared for the exhibition by Helen Luckett

Catalogue text by Roger Malbert

Catalogue designed by Karen Wilks
Printed by Amica Fine Art Print Limited, UK

Front cover: *Giant* (plate 4)

ISBN 1 85332 160 5

National Touring Exhibitions, Hayward Gallery and Arts Council Collection publications are distributed by Cornerhouse Publications, 70 Oxford Street, Manchester M1 5NH (tel. 0161 237 9662; fax. 0161 237 9664).

Preface

These eighteen etchings by Francisco Goya occupy a seminal place in the history of European graphic art. They were made at the beginning of the nineteenth century – printed on copper plates from England, of roughly the same size as those used by many English caricaturists of the period – yet they have lost none of their impact. They remain as powerful and relevant today as the prints of James Ensor, Pablo Picasso, George Grosz or Max Beckmann, all of whom were deeply influenced by Goya. This is one reason why we are including Goya in our series of smaller-scale National Touring Exhibitions, which tend otherwise to focus on modern or contemporary art and artists.

The Disparates are late works and, like other late works by great artists, they are not easily interpreted. They are best approached with some knowledge of Goya's earlier prints, but experience is rarely so methodically ordered. It is likely that many will encounter Goya here for the first time. The introduction and commentaries that follow are intended to suggest some ways in, although they give only a partial view of works which themselves represent a fraction of the artist's formidable output, and scarcely hint at his practice as a painter. It was largely in his prints and drawings, however, that Goya expressed his personal vision most freely, and *The Disparates* give a vivid glimpse into the mind of an extraordinary artist, described by André Malraux as 'the greatest interpreter of human anguish the West has known'.

Our thanks go to Antony Griffiths for his valuable advice and to Juliet Wilson-Bareau for her guidance on the commentaries.

Susan Ferleger Brades
Director
Hayward Gallery

Roger Malbert
Senior Curator, NTE
Hayward Gallery

Introduction

Goya was in his seventies when he made his last great series of etchings, some time between 1815 and 1823. He had been stone deaf since a serious illness in 1793, and he suffered a second near-fatal illness in 1819. The nature of the illnesses is uncertain, but their effect on his creative life is beyond question. Had he died in 1793, at the age of forty-seven, the Goya who has come down to us as the precursor of modern art, of Realism, Expressionism and Surrealism, the satirist and social critic, would scarcely have existed.

In 1819, after his second illness, Goya decorated the two main rooms of his house, known as the Quinta del Sordo (the house of the deaf man) with ferocious murals, the so-called 'black paintings'. Most of *The Disparates* were probably produced during the same period, for they are closely related in mood and imagery. Neither group of works saw the light of day until long after the artist's death in 1828. The 'black paintings' were first publicly exhibited in 1878 at the *Exposition Universelle* in Paris; *The Disparates* remained undiscovered for forty years after Goya went into exile in 1824, when he packed away the copperplates, together with other of his engravings, including the plates for *The Disasters of War* and albums of drawings, and stored them with his son. Unlike *The Disasters of War*, we have no edition of *The Disparates* numbered and titled by the artist to indicate their intended sequence and meaning. Only a few working proofs survive, of which fourteen have a short caption in Goya's hand, thirteen beginning with the word 'disparate', meaning 'folly' or 'absurdity'.

The Royal Academy of San Fernando made no reference to the existence of these proofs when it issued the first edition of eighteen of the prints posthumously in 1864 under the title *Los Proverbios*. By their – purely hypothetical – identification with popular Spanish proverbs, these strange, haunting images were supposedly explained, but no sure interpretation has ever been given and, like the 'black paintings', they remain obscure to this day.

A similar atmosphere of menace and diabolical, or comic, confusion pervades the paintings and the prints. Darkness is the overwhelming influence – the black of night. Yet as prints, *The Disparates* must have been conceived with some hope of public dissemination, if only within a small circle, and they are in fact highly entertaining. We are spared in them the bloody violence of the 'black paintings', dominated as these are by the twin pendants of *Saturn Devouring His Son* and *Judith and Holofernes*. Goya had already etched repeated scenes of murder, rape and pillage in *The Disasters of War*, completed in 1814. He himself must have tired of that relentless catalogue of human cruelty, for he digresses there, after sixty-five plates of literal reportage, into satire and allegory. Those last few plates in *The Disasters of War*, called by Goya *caprichos enfaticos* (emphatic caprices), provide one important link to *The Disparates*. Their place at the end of a series of depictions of acts of barbarism, such as he may well have witnessed, reminds us that Goya's melancholy is grounded in the experience of social, as well as personal, catastrophe.

After the War of Independence against the French, Spain saw two brief interludes of Liberal government, from 1812 to 1818 and again from 1820 to 1823. For the first time in Spanish history, the law rested not on the arbitrary power of Church and monarchy, but on a constitution. Universal (male) suffrage was introduced and the Inquisition was abolished. Some of Goya's closest friends were instrumental in accomplishing this release from despotism and feudalism, and there is no doubt where Goya's own sympathies lay. In 1823, the French invaded and returned to power the reactionary King Ferdinand VII. In the reign of terror that followed, the Inquisition was reintroduced and the Liberals purged – executed, gaoled or driven into exile. Goya himself went into hiding, until a general amnesty was declared and he was granted permission to leave for France, on the grounds of ill-health. Apart from two short visits to Madrid to petition for extensions to his leave, he never again set foot in Spain, dying in Bordeaux in 1828.

In the *caprichos enfaticos* the struggle against repression and religious fanaticism is represented through the metaphorical opposition of darkness and light. Truth, as a woman radiating light, is buried by monks while a priest blesses the corpse; as she is resurrected in the following image, a horrible shadowy crowd, including hooded monks, beats her down. Two plates earlier, a priest – in the drawing for this print wearing a papal crown – walks a tightrope; Goya's caption: *May the Rope Break*. If this and other images revealing the extent of the artist's cynicism and contempt for the Church had been known to the Inquisition, he would surely not have escaped unpunished.

Not all of Goya's satires are so direct. Under circumstances of severe censorship, the dissident artist may resort to subterfuge, veiling his message in allegory to confound the authorities. The notion of the dream, as a decentered narrative allowing the artist to express obliquely what he cannot openly declare, had a long tradition in eighteenth-century Spanish literature, and it was adopted by Goya in his initial plans for his first satirical etchings, eventually published under the title of *Los Caprichos* (caprices or fantasies) in 1799. The earliest prints in that series were entitled *Suenos* (dreams) and the drawing to plate number 43, which was to have served as the frontispiece and which bears the famous declaration 'the sleep of reason begets monsters', has the caption, *Universal Language*. The illogical world of dreams is captured in *The Caprichos* by the paradoxical interplay of words and images, the condensation of verbal and visual puns, of popular sayings, traditional symbols and his own wild inventions. Goya's 'universal language' was rarely wholly visual; almost all his drawings and prints after the mid-1790s bear captions and these are essential to his message.

The word 'disparate' occurs in Goya's work on only two occasions: on the thirteen proofs and in the caption to a drawing in the album of 1824-28. The Goya scholar Pierre Gassier remarks: 'So it would appear that this notion of disparate or "folly" only made its appearance very late in his work, and only after the great divide marked by his illness of 1819 – what I have called his "descent into hell"'. The drawing, *Gran Disparate*, shows a decapitated man being fed liquid through a funnel directly into his neck, an image adapted from Hieronymous Bosch's *Cure of Folly*, which Goya certainly knew from the Spanish royal collection. In fact, the word 'disparate' was frequently applied by older Spanish writers to Bosch's visionary compositions. A Spanish ecclesiastical commentator, writing in their defence in 1605, argued that they 'are not follies, but books of great prudence and artfulness, and if they are follies, they are our own, they are not his.' An objective, moralising intention can thus be attributed to Bosch's images (that is how they were protected from the Inquisition); however esoteric and fantastic, they are calmly composed and can be imagined at least to be capable of systematic decipherment, even if the key has now been lost.

Goya's *The Disparates*, on the other hand, seem too intensely subjective for any rational explanation. It is as if the artist were possessed by these demons and is struggling to control them – or is already in collusion with them. The impression of emotional turbulence can be felt in some of the preparatory drawings, whose tangled shapes contain a mass of barely discernible figures. There, the Goya of the 'black paintings' is at work, speaking a private language.

Among the many commentaries on Goya written in the past one hundred and fifty years, a short essay by Baudelaire remains one of the most illuminating. He had not seen *The Disasters of War* or *The Disparates* when, in 1857, he discussed Goya alongside Hogarth, Cruikshank and Bruegel, in 'Some Foreign Caricaturists'. Baudelaire had a philosophical interest in the question of laughter, and he saw Goya as representative of 'the eternal comic'. In uniting realism and fantasy, he had created 'a credible form of the monstrous':

> 'To the gaiety, the joviality, the typically Spanish satire of the "good old days" of Cervantes he unites a spirit far more modern, I mean a love of the ungraspable, a feeling for violent contrasts, for the blank horrors of nature and for human countenances weirdly animalised by circumstances.'

The Disparates are certainly the most 'ungraspable' of all Goya's prints, both because of the absence of definitive titles or commentaries, and because of the indeterminacy of the images themselves. Darkness makes for ambiguity; a shape can be interpreted in one way or in another. The ambiguity of these images extends to the shadows, where it is sometimes impossible to determine what is happening: a pair of wings, a uniformed man on horseback, a grinning phantom, a monster, half-human, half-animal, hovering in mid-flight. Goya was reported to have spoken often of 'the magic of the atmosphere of a picture' and, in *The Disparates*, aquatint is his means of mysteriously transforming a scene. It is necessary only to look at proofs made before and after the application of aquatint to appreciate its power. Goya's supreme command of this new technique – which was not available to Rembrandt – is demonstrated here in the subtle effects of night illuminated only by moonlight and the unstable flickering of flames. It is worth reflecting on this practical achievement to understand how these compelling images continue to grip us at the end of the twentieth century.

Goya always made drawings for his prints, usually in chalk and wash, and most of the drawings survive, with plate marks to show how they were run, moistened, through the press to transfer the image. Usually drawing and print correspond closely: the drawing having been reversed onto the plate, it comes out the original way round in the print. After transferring the image, Goya sometimes worked on the drawing again in wash, to sketch out areas of aquatint. But whereas an artist can rehearse an image in line drawing before it is transferred to the plate and then trace it from the original sketch, no such safe procedures exist for aquatint. Its effects cannot be simulated or exactly predicted; they belong to the process, to dust, resin and acid.

It has been suggested that Goya might have seen a show in Madrid of the new 'phantasmagoria', or magic lantern projections – an early version of cinema – at around the time when he was making *The Disparates*. This is possible, but it is as likely that he was inspired by dreams, actors on stage and the spectacle of carnival revelries and religious processions at night in city squares. Some of the scenes in *The Disparates* are set on a shallow stage, but most seem to take place out of doors at night, the figures engulfed in infinite space. Perhaps this sense of emptiness, of void, is part of what Baudelaire meant by the 'blank horrors of nature'. It is certainly one of the characteristically 'modern' aspects of Goya's world-view, indicative of his resolute materialism. 'Nature' for Goya rarely consists of more than a solitary tree, or a stump, a rock or a wall, for a setting. His only real interest is in human or animal nature.

Animal imagery is a traditional vehicle of graphic satire, and the owls, bats, goats, asses, cats and horses that appear in Goya's work are familiar from medieval woodcuts and eighteenth-century English political caricatures. More powerful, however, and more disturbing, is Goya's confusion of the human and the animal, not just by the transplantation of the head of one species onto the body of another, but by the emphasis on the bestial in the human – the effect observed by Baudelaire.

Animal or puppet – these variations on the human always seem to be present in Goya, whether subtly inflected, as in the commissioned painted portraits, or accentuated, as they are in his imaginative works. Behind the animal lurks the monstrous, and behind the din of voices, silence. The soundlessness of *The Disparates* is almost palpable, and in the absence of sound, sense too disappears, for there is no sense without discourse, of which speech is the greater part. It is hard not to impute to Goya's deafness an enormous influence in heightening his visual powers – to imagine his intense isolation, as he witnessed cacophonous scenes of war and carnival, deaf to the cries or laughter of the people he depicts so vividly.

Goya's realism springs from observation of the life around him. He continued to draw until his death; as an old man in Bordeaux, he sketched street performers, crippled beggars on their makeshift carts, a condemned man at the guillotine. These drawings are mingled with fantasies and caricatures, of witches, hooded monks, penitents, prisoners, flying animals and disembodied heads. Among them is one that can be taken to express Goya's own spirit, of a bearded old man on sticks with a look of fierce determination and the caption, *I Am Still Learning*.

Roger Malbert

Principal Sources

P. Gassier, *The Drawings of Goya (1) The Complete Albums*, Thames & Hudson Ltd, London, 1973; *(II) The Sketches, Studies and Individual Drawings*, Thames & Hudson Ltd, London, 1975

P. Gassier, J. Wilson and F. Lachenal, *Goya, His Life and Work*, Thames & Hudson Ltd, Fribourg and London, 1971

T. Harris, *Goya. Engravings and Lithographs*, 2 vols., Cassirer, Oxford, 1964

F.D. Klingender, *Goya and the Democratic Revolution*, Sidgwick & Jackson Ltd, London, 1948, repbl. 1968

F. Licht, *Goya in Perspective*, Prentice, New Jersey, 1973

A.E. Perez Sanchez et al, *Goya and the Spirit of Enlightenment*, Little, Brown & Company, Madrid, Boston, New York, 1989

J. Wilson-Bareau, *Goya's Prints*, British Museum Press, London, 1996

J. Wilson-Bareau and E. Santiago, *Ydioma Universal: Goya e la Biblioteca Nacional*, Biblioteca Nacional, Madrid, 1996

All of Goya's print series are reproduced at actual size, in paperback, published by Dover:

Los Caprichos, New York, 1969
The Disasters of War, New York, 1967
La Tauromaquia and The Bulls of Bordeaux, New York, 1969
The Disparates or *The Proverbios*, New York, 1969

Related Illustrations

The illustrations on pages 12–17 are referred to in the introduction; those following relate to the plates.

Asmodea *c*.1820-23
oil on plaster, 123 x 265cm
Prado Museum, Madrid

The Great He-Goat (El Gran Cabron) *c*.1820-23
oil on plaster, 140 x 438cm
Prado Museum, Madrid

14

Truth has Died (Murió la Verdad) *c.*1815-20
red chalk, 14.6 x 20.3cm
drawing for *The Disasters of War*, plate 79
Prado Museum, Madrid

Nothing. The Event Will Tell (Nada. Ello dirá) *c.*1812-20
etching and aquatint, 15.5 x 20cm
The Disasters of War, plate 69
photograph © British Museum 1997

Divine Liberty!
(Divina Libertad) *c.*1814-23
indian ink and sepia wash, 20.6 x 14.4cm
Prado Museum, Madrid

May the Rope Break (Que se rompe la cuerda) *c.*1815-20
red chalk, 14.5 x 20.3cm
drawing for *The Disasters of War*, plate 77
Prado Museum, Madrid

Great Folly
(Gran Disparate) *c*.1824-28
black chalk, 19.2 x 15.2cm
Prado Museum, Madrid

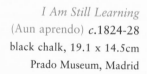

I Am Still Learning
(Aun aprendo) *c*.1824-28
black chalk, 19.1 x 14.5cm
Prado Museum, Madrid

Self Portrait *c.*1815
oil on canvas, 46 x 35cm
Prado Museum, Madrid

The Straw Mannequin
(El Pelele) **1791-92**
oil on canvas, 267 x 160cm
Prado Museum, Madrid

Feminine Folly (Disparate feminino) *c.*1815-24
red chalk and sanguine wash, 23.2 x 33.2cm
drawing for *The Disparates*, plate 1
Prado Museum, Madrid

What a Tailor Can Do!
(¡Lo que puede un Sastre!) **1797-98**
red chalk and sanguine wash, 23.8 x 16.3cm
drawing for *The Caprichos*, plate 52
Prado Museum, Madrid

Fearful Folly *c.*1815-24
red chalk and sanguine wash, 23.3 x 33.1cm
drawing for *The Disparates*, plate 2
Prado Museum, Madrid

Ridiculous Folly (Disparate ridiculo) *c.*1815-24
sanguine wash, 22.7 x 32cm
drawing for *The Disparates*, plate 3
Prado Museum, Madrid

*Giant c.*1815-24
red chalk and sanguine wash, 24.2 x 32.5cm
Drawing for *The Disparates*, plate 4
Prado Museum, Madrid

Bon Voyage (Buen Viage) **1797-98**
etching, burnished aquatint and burin
21.8 x 15.2cm
The Caprichos, plate 64
photograph © British Museum 1997

Cruel Folly (Disparate cruel) *c.*1815-24
red chalk and sanguine wash, 24.4 x 35.4cm
drawing for *The Disparates*, plate 6
Prado Museum, Madrid

Will No One Untie Us?
(¿No hay quien nos desate?) **1797-98**
etching and aquatint, 21.7 x 15.2cm
The Caprichos, plate 75
photograph © British Museum 1997

Dream of Lying and Inconstancy 1797-98
pen and sepia ink with wash
drawing for *The Caprichos*
Prado Museum, Madrid

Figures Enveloped in Sacks c.1815-24
sanguine wash, 24.1 x 32.5cm
drawing for *The Disparates*, plate 8
Prado Museum, Madrid

General Folly (Disparate general) *c.*1815-24
red chalk and sanguine wash, 23 x 33cm
drawing for *The Disparates*, plate 9
Prado Museum, Madrid

Fierce Monster (Fiero monstruo!) *c.*1815-20
etching, drypoint and burin, 17.5 x 22cm
The Disasters of War prepared for plate 81 but not published
photograph © British Museum 1997

Poor Folly (Disparate pobre) *c.*1815-24
red chalk and sanguine wash, 24 x 33.5cm
drawing for *The Disparates*, plate 11
Prado Museum, Madrid

Blind Man's Buff 1788-89
oil on canvas, 269 x 350cm
Prado Museum, Madrid

Commentaries

The eighteen prints here, etched between 1816 and 1824, were included in the first edition published posthumously in 1864 by the Royal Academy of San Fernando. Four further copper plates were later discovered, and there is evidence that there were more to the series, which was probably left incomplete by Goya. The sequence here is that chosen (arbitrarily) for the first edition. Titles other than Goya's own are given in square brackets.

All the prints are the same size, 24.5 cm x 35 cm (height before width). They were etched on the same batch of English copper plates as Goya's bullfighting series, *Tauromaquia*, published in 1816.

Sources for the following commentaries include Gassier (1975), Perez Sanchez et al (1989) and Wilson-Bareau (1996).

1. *Feminine Folly*
This recalls the early tapestry cartoon, *El Pelele* (The Mannequin) of 1791-92, depicting the same theme, but in a lighter mood. In the drawing for this print, four women hold the blanket, which seems to contain a human figure, but not the donkey; behind, to the right, a crowd watches the scene.

2. *[Fearful Folly]*
The title was invented by one of Goya's biographers. Goya often depicted hooded and cloaked figures, such as monks and old women. This image relates to two of *The Caprichos*: number 3, *Here Comes the Bogeyman*, and number 52, *What a Tailor Can Do!*, where a dead tree draped in a friar's habit looms over a group of fearful figures who kneel in worship before it. In *Fearful Folly*, the soldiers scrambling away in terror recall similar groups of figures in *The Disasters of War*. In the

drawing for this print, the figure on the ground clasps his hands in supplication. Note the little face looking out of the sleeve.

3. *Ridiculous Folly*

A cloaked figure presides over a group perched high on the dead branch of a tree, including two veiled women and a bearded man who appears to have nodded off. All except the speaker have their hands covered, which has led some interpreters to suggest that this is a satire on the Spanish aristocracy – the hidden hands signifying their uselessness, the branch an allusion to family trees.

4. [*Giant*]

Gigantism was a favourite theme of Goya's, often with a threatening aspect. Here, a grinning giant dances with castanets before two figures. In the drawing and an earlier state of this print the man crouching behind a religious effigy wears a friar's habit. On either side of the giant, spectral faces loom out of the darkness.

5. *Flying Folly*

The grinning hybrid monster, half horse and half bird, can be compared with similar creatures in *The Caprichos* numbers 19 and 48, and the scene of flying witches in *Buen Viage*, *The Caprichos* number 64. The woman seems to be carried away against her will, her hands raised in helpless alarm.

6. *Cruel Folly*

This composition recalls the stark encounters of *The Disasters of War*, except for the grotesquely comic element of the crouching figure. He does not appear in the drawing, where the armed man wields a musket rather than a lance and in the background there is a sentry box, instead of a ruined wall. In shadow, a fleeing figure, like the screaming woman in *Poor Folly* (plate 11), evokes an atmosphere of terror.

7. *Disorderly Folly*

These weird siamese twins, one male and one female, can be compared with the double-headed man in plate 16, the couple struggling to free themselves in *The Caprichos* number 75, *Will No One Untie Us?*, and the two-faced woman in the print, *Dream of Lying and Inconstancy*. The gathering is similar to the witches' sabbath in the 'black painting', *The Great He-Goat*.

8. [*Men in Sacks*] or [*Aristocrats*]

This enigmatic image suggests the vanity and pretensions of the aristocracy (see plate 3) or perhaps the sacks are connected with penitential rituals. The three men to the right of the erect figure seem to be inspecting – enviously, admiringly or mockingly – the bulge in his sack.

9. *General Folly*

Two hideous characters, one in clerical robes, kneel before a family of cats nesting in the shawl of a grotesque figure, wearing what could be carnival costume. Behind, a woman and a flailing baby seem to be borne away by a clutch of indeterminate figures into darkness. Below them, a Rembrandtesque bearded old man studies a book.

10. [*Woman Carried Off By a Horse*]

The horse, conventionally emblematic of unbridled desire, tosses a vacantly-smiling woman into the air. Another woman in the background seems to be climbing into the mouth of a horrible beast, like a giant rat or dog, that recalls the *Cruel Monster* in one of the additional plates to *The Disasters of War*. In the more explicitly allegorical drawing, a man is dragged along by the horse.

11. *Poor Folly*

Old women in shawls, typical celestinas, grooming or advising young women in the ways of love and the world, are common in Goya's graphic works. Here the young woman has two heads, one apparently straining forward to hear the words of her elders, the other turning to see the deathly figure pursuing her. The drawing is quite different.

12. *Merry Folly*

This circle of revellers dancing with castanets has its origins in one of Goya's early tapestry cartoons, *Blind Man's Buff*, 1786. The dwarfish old men are dressed in the fashionable costumes of the *majo*, a lower class 'tough' of the time, and the women wear luxurious versions of Spanish national dress.

13. *A Way of Flying*

This is the one title given by Goya that does not begin with the word 'disparate'. This print may be the earliest in the series, for it was included in a special set of *Tauromaquia*, as published in 1816.

14. *Carnival Folly*

The two clownish men clutching their groins are entertaining an assembly of leering onlookers. Other carnivalesque figures, including one on stilts, cavort around them. The reclining figure in the centre recalls the French soldiers in many of *The Disasters of War* and suggests a hidden political meaning in the scene.

15. *Evident Folly*

This print was altered substantially between early and later states. In the former, the demonic-looking priest points into a fiery abyss. In this later state, the flames are replaced by a soldier plunging headlong into a pit. The heavy awning supported by figures standing on each other's shoulders threatens to collapse, plunging the entire assembly into darkness.

16. [*Indecision*]

What kind of advice or admonition is being offered to the three-handed man who tilts his head as if he were hard of hearing? With one right hand he holds his hat, but he has another stretched out behind him, tugged at by a beseeching woman. She in turn is linked to a chain of figures. Several faces, leering, grinning or squinting – perhaps variations of the same face – sprout from the figures on the left, including one on the elbow of the old woman in white. In the background a barely distinguishable figure seems to be bound to a tree.

17. [*Man Being Mocked*]

In the drawing for this print, the central figure is a tall man standing solemnly in a hieratic pose, with arms crossed over his chest.

18. [*Old Man Confronting Demons*]

The swarm of spirits flying to greet their new companion as he emerges from the recumbant body (either sleeping or dead) is shrouded in darkness, yet the familiar forms of hobgoblins and grinning monsters can be made out. Some of them hover absurdly a few feet off the ground as if suspended over a pantomime stage. The more distant spirits are almost lost in the gloom. The face of the emerging spirit might well be Goya's. The image may be compared with *The Caprichos* number 43, *The Sleep of Reason Produces Monsters*. It has been suggested that this *Disparate*, which has no caption in Goya's hand, was intended to be the frontispiece to the series.

Plates

1. *Feminine Folly* (Disparate feminino)
etching, aquatint and drypoint

2. *Fearful Folly*
etching, burnished aquatint and drypoint

3. *Ridiculous Folly* (Disparate ridiculo) etching, aquatint and drypoint

4. *Giant*
etching, burnished aquatint, durin and drypoint

5. *Flying Folly* (Disparate volante)
etching and aquatint

6. *Cruel Folly* (Disparate cruel)
etching and burnished aquatint

7. *Disorderly Folly* (Disparate desordenado)
etching, aquatint and drypoint

8. *Men in Sacks* or *Aristocrats*
etching and burnished aquatint

9. *General Folly* (Disparate general)
etching and burnished aquatint

10. *Woman Carried Off By a Horse*
etching, burnished aquatint and drypoint

11. *Poor Folly* (Disparate pobre) etching, burnished aquatint, drypoint and burin

12. *Merry Folly* (Disparate Allegre)
etching, burnished aquatint and drypoint

13. *A Way of Flying* (Modo de volar)
etching, aquatint and drypoint

14. *Carnival Folly* (Disparate de carnabal)
etching and aquatint

15. *Evident Folly* (Disparate claro)
etching, burnished aquatint and lavis

16. *Indecision*
etching and burnished aquatint

17. *Man Being Mocked*
etching and burnished aquatint

18. *Old Man Confronting Demons*
etching, burnished aquatint and burin

laughter / comic

Schadenfreude

alienated - worried when figures
           are inhumane

genius, playful
games become sinister
and sinister, dark actions become
                   less like a game.